WANDER

By

Henry Hoover

For everyone who never felt

"good enough"

For everyone who never

"fit in"

Smile, because you are and you do.

Dear Reader,

I hope that you enjoy this book of poetry; volume two of three in the trilogy: "Three Mysteries/Three Miracles". The poetry that follows is a summer storm; it is waves crashing in the sea, it is the water on the wind, it is snow gently gliding. From wondering comes wandering when one knows not where to go, when one feels alone. Angrier, sadder, more volatile and at the same time peaceful and content, Wander will take you from a state of reflection to sudden introspective interrogation. Without further ado, I give you Wander.

Love, Henry

Table of Contents

- Let Me Just Say- 5
- My Cataclysm- 8
- Love Is Empty- 9
- I Think It's Time- 12
- Strange Air- 13
- Fleeting- 16
- Liars- 18
- Bruised Thighs...-20
- Being Speared- 21
- From The Day...-25
- Break- 30
- Smile- 34
- I'm Not Sure- 37
- No, Baby- 44
- I Want- 59
- CHANGING- 53
- Savior- 54
- GROWING- 55
- The Principle...- 56
- Blue Plaid- 63
- BEAUTIFUL- 64
- Lay Bricks- 65
- Broken Back- 69
- Map- 76
- GOLD- 77
- Seventeen- 78
- Don't Miss Out- 83
- IN THE PAST- 86
- DON'T BE- 87
- Change- 88
- YOUR HEART- 95
- Set In Stone- 96
- TIME IS NOW- 98
- A Little Bit Older- 99
- Currently...- 100
- Fearfully Afraid- 104
- Say This Once- 108
- Weight...-120
- Truth In Lies...-122
- The World Is...-135
- From...-138
- Ask Me- 140
- Fairytales- 144
- Measure- 146
- Compass- 147
- Mongolia- 149
- Here- 150
- Sinking Into...- 151
- Brother- 153
- Your Dove - 155
- Tell Me- 157
- Take Me...- 158
- Sublime- 160
- Sour Milk- 162
- Youth- 164

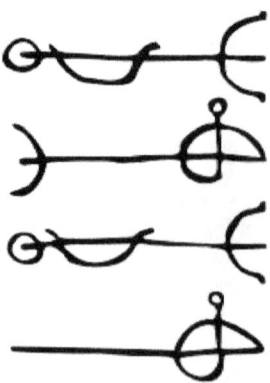

Let Me Just Say

Let me just say

Whether or not you hear me

Whether or not I speak

Let me just say

You make it difficult

You make things difficult

Loving you was never difficult

Naturally, it came

Like breathing, it came

Naturally, it just was

That was then

This is now

Now, let me just say

I'm not sorry

I'm not sorry for getting upset

I'm not sorry for going away

Let Me Just Say

I'm sorry you didn't try harder

Let me just say

I've never thought much of myself

But when I look back and I *will* look back

On all that ever was

(Between us)

I will see that I am worth

So

Much

More

Than how you made me feel

I felt like gold most of the time

Scratch that

Some of the time

I told you

You were gold

I showed you

You are gold

Let Me Just Say

But I was always silver

I was always bronze

Your smile no longer makes me melt

The sweltering heat has subsided

What is left?

I see you for what you are

I see me for what I am

Now

Let me just say

This time

I am not coming back

I am not calling back

This time is the last time

And next time

I'll be gone

My Cataclysm

My cataclysm

Something deep

Sad

Like water

The calmest

Place

Is often

Deepest

Right or left

Or maybe in-between

The hardest steps to take

Are often hardly seen

Love Is Empty

Love is empty

Stretched and

Clean

In the sun

It hangs

From linen

String

In the wind

Twists and

Tumbles

Love is empty

Stretched and

Clean

Your hand's touch

His or hers

At night I

Forget

[9]

Love Is Empty

From where I

Came

In the sun

I hang

From linen

String

In the wind

I stagger,

Hurt

I am empty

Stretched and

Clean

I gasp and

Shudder

When all becomes

Still

Stare at the ceiling

And I become

Still

Love Is Empty

My skin, it burns

But burns

For what

I gasp and shudder

When all becomes

Still

For empty

Stretched

And clean love

My skin

Desires

It

Requires

Strength

Perseverance

And

Will

I Think It's Time

I think it's time

i think it right

No longer shall i

Capitalize

My eyes

i think it's near

Through thick and thin

No longer shall i

Capitalize

My i's

I'll say we,

Yes, you and me

I'll say him and her

They'll forget the I'll

In mounds of dirt

And mourn him

When they remember

[12]

Strange Air

Breathe in

This strange air

Residual feelings

Come and go

Look in the mirror

Once, twice, and

Third time's

A charm

Charming to think

Of happier days passed

Of those still to come

Fly away, fly away

Don't look back, not once

Bite your lip and roll your eyes

But don't look back, not once

Dirt on skin, stretched on bone

Dirty feelings, come and go

Strange Air

These residual feelings

They come and go

Paint yourself blue

Not unlike ocean, sky, or sea

Vessels move across, within

Emotion creates current

Voices stir, pull my hair

Twenty after

Forty 'til

This strange air surrounds

These feelings resound

And at the end of the day

All's fair

Fleeting

Everything is so fleeting

Time and touch

This world seems

To know no bounds

But still

It's all so fleeting

Perhaps

Fleeting isn't

The right word

Perhaps

Changing

Everything is so

Everything seems so

Everything is so

Changing

Full of change

Fleeting

On the brink of

Change

Everything is

Everything will be

Everything is

Light

Fleeting

Changing

But most importantly

Light

Liars

Liars just

Lie to me

Soft and sweet

With

A bite

Spread your noxious

Words upon

My barren body

Tell me what you are doing

Tell me where and when

Tell me that you love me

But that there simply

Isn't time to

Spend. Mend.

Comprehend.

You will hurt me,

Break me, bare down

Upon my already

Liars

Unstable spinal column

With every lie

That spills forth

From your mouth

Like sea foam during a storm

Words are whispered back and forth

Understood but not put forth

Eyes can set, lock, look away

Week after week, day after day

And smiles flash

Over teeth so white

But I know it's because

You bleach them at night

I drink down your lies

They are saturated

Beneath my skin

And it hurts. Fuck, does it hurt.

But I allow it. I allow it.

I allow it.

Just know, I know.

Bruised Thighs, Black Eyes

Transition is not

My transgression

Rather my

Transcendence

Storm clouds illuminate

Stormy weather

Instigates

Blue skies like

Bruised thighs

Locked and closed

Open skies

Black eyes

With a mouth

Half closed

Lips trembling

Quiver, hold

That sob inside

Hold that storm

Bruised Thighs, Black Eyes

From days of youth

Growing old

Words embrace

Can slip and slither

Others, like arrows

Break ribs

Pierce lungs

Stormy, hollow

Trains of thought

Golden rays

Clear, cloudless days

Trace your steps

All the way

Back to the beginning

And further still

Only to find

What you knew

Was already

There

Being Speared

I sit on metal

Sit on stone

Stare at stone

Stare at metal

Infinite blue

A chasm of sky

If I were to ever escape

I'd flee to the stars

I walk on stone

Occasionally tar

And marvel at the concept

We dig into the Earth

For Her black blood

And then bury it again

A blood transfusion

For our boats and cars

Being Speared

We don't mind

The redundancy

And when we cut

Her deep

Our mother Earth

We let her blood

Poor into the seas

Windy weather

Bloody tides

While we sit

Idly by

And if storms do muster

Above waves of black

Her blood will paint our houses

Paint our walls

Our faces

And the pseudo innocent

Will be doused in

The sins of others

Being Speared

The wrongs of others

Still, we chase that dollar bill

And trudge through

An oil spill

We all sleep well

At night

Toss and turn

Dreams that burn

Yeah we all sleep well

At night

And maybe

A few of us

Maybe we hurt like Her

Maybe all we do

Is gush

Maybe Jesus and the Earth

Lock arms and talk about

Being speared

From The "Day by Day"

Politics of day by day

Motions to the week

Month

Industry

Vessels and empty devices

Repeating each motion

Exterior decaying

Exterior eroding with

Time while time grips

Pulls, rips pieces

Of armor and steel

And politics of day by day

They dance in circles

They dance

And decay

Their currents and flurries and maelstroms

Pull you asunder

From The "Day by Day"

Pull your breath under

All goes blue

Cascading white light

Day by day

This isn't here

This is there

And there

And there

No, this isn't here

This is

Everywhere.

But know your vessel

Sentient being

Chains will shatter

Decay will progress into

Growth

Wondrous growth

From The "Day by Day"

And the daily dance

Of made-up words

And circumstance

It will fade

It will become the future

You have made

Time no longer

Rips and wounds

But softly, whispered

Pushes against you

Pushes against you

Not with force,

But with a gentle kindness

Saying "Here is not good for you,

You're growing, you're learning"

Saying "You're hurting, but here is not good for you

You cannot give up"

Saying "You still have tomorrow,

From The "Day by Day"

Next month,

10 years from now,

20 minutes from now."

Saying "Make best of what you have right now, always,

Make best of what you will have then, always."

Saying "The future is bright"

Saying "You cannot give up now"

And the politics of day by day

The beige walls and crème Brule

The stunted whispers

And feigned pearly whites

The sex-appeal

And self-appeal,

The lies that twist and toil

The truths that never spoil

They will be wasted away

They will have wasted away

However, were not wasted.

From The "Day by Day"

They will follow suit

They will fall

Into a metamorphoses

Transform

Transcend

And politics of the "day by day"

Yes, they will

Fade away

Turning into

Brilliant colors

Turning into you

Convalescing you

Cry

Weep

Smile

Laugh

With honesty

Be bored with honesty

Eat food

Drink coffee

From The "Day by Day"

With honesty

Break forth

From the "day by day"

Breathe forth.

Break forth.

And make this dream, make your dreams

Make them your hours, your days

Your industry

Break

Tremble

At night

Under darkness

Under blankets

Beneath sheets

Tremble

Scratch

Grip the mattress

Palms down

Nails digging

Deep

Tremble

With every minute

That passes

With every thought

With every thought

Break

Tremble

For your past

And present

Tremble

For what others

What they think of you

Tremble for whom

You know you are

And the chasm

That lies between

The two

Tremble

For all

You want to do

But can't

Tremble

For all you want to be

But can't.

Break

Because catching

A bullet

And chasing your dreams

Yes, these

Truly

Are two things

Are two things

You can want to do

But can't.

Wait in silence

Realize

These are two

Things you want

To do but can't

Because weakness

Is a glimmer

Is a shimmer

Break

In your touch

Can't pull a trigger

Can't pick up a brush

Wait in silence

Realize

Can't is

Can't is

Can't was

Always taught

To be far

From your vocabulary

You can

You can

You will.

And you have chosen

Break/pick up a brush

Smile

Thoughts of truth

Not fiction, fact

Thoughts that push me

Thoughts that scare

Can't breathe

And day to day

I look at the sky

When I can't breathe

I look at the sky

Thoughts of truth,

Not fiction, fact

Ideas that envelope me

Take me inside

Fists clench

From time to time

Smile

Toes clench, too

I just can't breathe

Now and then

Now again

Sun comes out

Blue sky ray

Breathe deep

Once, twice

Breathe deep

Smile.

Sometimes

It only takes a smile

To remember why you

Smile

Every day

Sometimes

It only takes a smile

Smile

To remember why you

Sigh in dismay

Sometimes

It only takes the effort

To smile when

You really don't want to

The effort

To do

What you want to do

But really don't

Want to.

It only takes a smile.

Breathe; one, two.

Smile; one, two.

Especially during

Those times

You really

Don't want to.

I'm Not Sure

Honestly, I wake up

Stumble, deep breath

I know just where

My steps will lead

Naked, I shower

Naked, shoulders low

Head hanging low

Every day, I know

Steam fills my lungs

Deep sighs, thoughts tug

But every day, hope

Like liquid gold

Spills down my spine

White washes

Cleanses

Bad thoughts

I'm Not Sure

Painful memories

Every day, not

Every morning

Though morning glory

Waves of worry

Throw my motion

Into a whirlpool

Spinning commotion

Bathroom tile

Clean, clean floor

Stare at the ceiling

Above

Can't hope for more

Clean love, like

Linen, stained.

My body shudders

Pulse quickens

I'm Not Sure

Hope is eternal

But so, I fear,

Is my internal

Insurrection

A void, like razor

Against flesh

Or glass

Against flesh

Or jagged glints

Of mineral, stone

Against

Pale, tender flesh

I feel alone

Lies I've told

Truths behold

A greater truth

Known

Words are whispered

Softly carried

I'm Not Sure

To the ceiling

From the bathroom

Tile floor

My past

Present

Future

Memories, dreams are

Precious pearls

Cast before swine

But at times

Chosen, thought

To be benign

Just another self-told

Lie.

Still, I whisper

Shudder, free

My thoughts

They drift

I'm Not Sure

To you, or

He.

Never her,

Though she hurts,

Aggravates, frustrates.

Never her.

Or maybe

Now and then

They drift to you

And all

Who've made me

Trip or fall

But on the bathroom

Tile floor

I want all of you

Maybe more

I want all of this

I'm Not Sure

Maybe more

I believe all of this

Maybe more

And foggy haze

Find your way

I keep my demons,

Left at bay,

I hum my worries

All away

And focus on

The hope

Like dripping

Glorious

Molten gold

Running down my spine

Down my spine

And let my thoughts

Drift

My whispered

I'm Not Sure

Words lift

I allow my thoughts

To sail

On waves

To shores

Of your

Face, smile

Hot, heavy

Being, glow

Hope is pure

But of outcomes

I'm never sure.

Maybe

Possibly

I hope

This time I'm

Certain.

Grand.

No, Baby

Now

We lay in the grass

We were painting

And we were acting

I acted like I could paint

You acted like

There was more

On your mind

Than what was

On your mind

I remember the colors

And watching you smile

I photographed it

Listening to you speak

You ruined

A canvas of mine

With your sincere proof

No, Baby

Proving that you

In reality

Could not paint

I was happy

I remember

Or, I thought I was

Crawdads In the creek

My mother told me

Tie bacon to a string

Raw bacon

And they'll eat it

Too many ways

To catch a crawdad

I wanted to catch you

But people are different

Love is different

I thought I had

But I was wrong.

No, Baby

Fast-forward

5 years stronger

5 years strong

God, I never knew

A love so long

So wrong

Now gone,

And I'm happy.

Fuck, am I happy.

Now, I paint

Mentally deliberate

And appreciate

Every day with a

Surreal splendor

Seldom seen

Now, I knew

Just what you meant

No, Baby

You were in the grass

You painted a tree

Two paths

To go down,

One bright, one true

The other diseased

And hurt; always

Hurting.

I'm bright, I'm blue

And with every

Step I take

I'm closer to

Truth

I know

I'm where I'm meant to be

And you're going

To a place you've prepared

But the sorrow I thought

No, Baby

Would arise from the start

It's far from me.

That day, I tried

To grab your hand

Lay my head on your chest

No, baby. Not today.

You simply painted

I had finished. You

Hadn't. The sun went

Down and the day

Became a memory

The place you've prepared, I know

Like fire, burns

Caution blows on whispering winds

Now, 5 years

Growing, 5 years gone

I'm so happy.

I Want

I want a pool of water

Fire, pain

Clear these days away

I want pure

Drip drop

Clean white sheets

Morning light

On your face

I want a smile

Without break

I want clouds

And blue skies

Surround

I want to rise

Above, I want

I Want

To forget who I am

I want

To settle down

I want to be

This way forever

I wish death would

Come for me

I wish it would

Envelope me

I wish I could wake

Up in your arms and

Live forever

I wish I wasn't like this

I wish this wasn't my

Reflection

I Want

I wish God above

Would pity me

A grace with your

Hand held high

More over,

I wish I could fly

I wish you would lean

In and whisper soft

It will all be ok

These things

They end up this way

But I want you to know

It'll be ok

I want to be alone

I never want to be alone

Again

I want to play hopscotch

I Want

On I-35

And win.

Birds fly above,

High above,

I want to play hopscotch

On I-35

Noon sun, shadows cast

And win.

It'll be ok.

I'll close my eyes

To the water's line

It will be ok.

EVERYTHING

IS

CHANGING

Savior

Stuck and need

Could you please

Come help me in the night

Lying awake

Cold, eyes wide

Mind's eye holds you in sight

Don't tumble, don't tremble

Don't cast me away

For things over which I've no control

Just hold me, just keep me

'Til morning's light

When I can stand up on my own

Just lead me, just guide

A beacon so bright

'Til I can stand up on my own

Forgive me, just give me

One more night

So I can stand up on my own

EVERYTHING

IS

GROWING

☾

The Principle Business of Life

I saw storm clouds

A moon's soft glow

I was alone

And wanted you to know

Textbook, soft book

Nestled between

Far off looks

And the waiter

Came to take my food away

I asked for

My check

It had been

A rough day

The Principle Business of Life

He handed it to me

Gently, from his

Breast pocket

He handed it to me

Swiftly, I forced

A smile, shudder, hold,

I asked him for

A fortune cookie

He brought two.

I was alone

And wanted you to know

I ate my fortune

Keeper's crypt

Read it aloud

In my mind

It read:

The Principle Business of Life

"The principle business of life

Is to enjoy it."

I put it in

My breast pocket.

Drove away, drove home

I was alone, and

Wanted you to know.

Beneath waves

Of water cold

I open my eyes

Only to behold

Distorted visions

Of a reality

A mold only to behold

My life in its closing

And I beheld

The Principle Business of Life

In shaking hands

I held fire

And in shaking breaths

I took in water.

Closed my eyes,

White away

And tomorrow's

Flicker came with

Furrowed brows.

My 2nd fortune cookie,

I saved for a day

I drove in the sun

I hadn't meant to be late

But my mind has been

In such a sorry state

I had no other choice

The Principle Business of Life

Than to walk

Torturously, tenderly

And mentally debate.

My fortune filled my mouth

Cracked pale paper

Tasted sweet

And words bled, ink bled

Into my retinas

They said:

"Where there is an open mind,

There will always be a frontier"

Fortunate morning

For sleep was kind

Wrapped its arms around me

I didn't have to think

No, nothing on my mind

The Principle Business of Life

Between the world and I

Shaking fear; between

People and I

Disappear

At times, I feel

I'm heterotopic

My world melts,

I don't belong

And when I see

I'm homotopic

My map unfolds

And joins another

My map unfolds

I'm not grey matter

In the cerebral lobe

No, I love.

The Principle Business of Life

My love wants to join another

From above

My map wants to

Know another

A foreign dove

My fortune cookies

They tasted sweet

Now fill my mouth

And mind with distaste

The time I spend exploring

Seems a waste

I'm homoeotic

And homotopic

And will rest

When my map

Joins another.

Blue Plaid

Blue plaid

Afternoon sun

Afternoon light

Overhead glints

Through trees

Or leaves

On steps

Grey smoke

Back brace

Present my case

It's not too far to go

Not far at all

EVERYTHING

IS

BEAUTIFUL

Lay Bricks

Tragic.

You walk back and forth

Down the same corridors

Every single day

And though your rhythms

May be resistant to change

Your "self" becomes distant

Fades to rearrange.

Tragedy in subtle sighs

The sound of palms

Passing you by

More and more

Your eyes are glued

To the concrete

More and more

Lay Bricks

Your map with pins

Of all the places you will

Go and grow

Is becoming heavy

With days you can only wait

And know

And the patience

That once was your gold

Filled glass figurine,

In the shape of a butterfly

Or a basking fish

A lark about to fly

Away, your patience

That was once bestowed

Upon you has started to erode

Tragic. You're not becoming

Volatile or belligerent

Lay Bricks

Not angry or hopeless.

No; but as the tides change

As your being fades to rearrange

You're becoming cold

Alone

Laying bricks upon bricks

Mortar made of blood

And sweat

And you swear

It's necessary

And you thought

You hoped

For someone to share

Some of your burden or cares

You dared hope

But it was not so.

So, you lay bricks

With mortar made of your blood

And sweat

Lay Bricks

And you swear

Keeping others 40 yards away

Locked in your cellar

Every single day

As the corridors you walk through

Accumulate dust

Your value in life

And more than you know

Morning to night

Has begun to grow cold

And you swear

Laying bricks from dusk 'til

Dawn will, you hope, heal your

Wears and tears and hold others away

When you were little

You'd watch water swirl down a drain;

Now the water's all gone

Broken Back

Standing in line;

Wal-Mart. Quarter past 5,

And you'll be somewhere else

Somewhere safe

Where you can slave

Away

Wearing a crescent moon

Smile, caught by gentle sighs

The sky is an image

Of perfection

Seeping into your brain

And you suddenly realize

You aren't capable

Of maintaining

Or, no,

You won't

Complain

Broken Back

But broken

Backed don't

Step in those cracks

Your mother

Your poor mother

You'll break her back, too

And all those tears

That bend your soul forward

Will burn an image of

Pain and furrowed brows

If you dare stumble

Into those cracks

Broken bones

In slumber

Moan, of times

Since passed

Grown cold

Cold, nostalgic

Mornings true

Broken Back

Sip hot water

Leaves steep

For a minute's length

And 10 past nine

You'll be in a different

Set of walls, ceiling

Floor

With words and whispers

A landscape shorn

Different and every hour

On the dot

Eyelids crease

In distant thought

Broken backed

Forlorn glances

Who is your straw?

Who broke your heart?

(Or back)

(Or ribs)

Broken Back

(Or knees)

(Or wrists)

You wear a gentle smile

For everyone you greet

Some of whom you meet

And hope for the best

For humanity

And all the rest

You hope for the best

For every face you see

Prove your love

In your thoughts

When hoping

All the people

You see

Aren't like you

That they are, or

Come to be

Broken Back

Happy

But at night,

Strip yourself bare

Hand on back

Rubbing

Scratching

Who's going to help

Mend you?

What's going to help

Mend you?

Coffee shop setting

11 'til 12

You: still by yourself

Got to push forward

Go to that mental place

Of strength or well being

Watch all of the people

Broken Back

Smile, laugh, talk, and embrace

Wonder when you'll

Achieve your grace

To not wonder

Whose hand will

Fall into yours

Or whose shoulders will be beauty-shed

Full of soft, white

Light in the morning

In your bed

Go forward with your

Life, time to leave things

Unsaid

Rake leaves of different

Colors and do the same

For thoughts

Into a pile, for black bags

Or mulch

Broken Back

And drive forward

Push forward

Like your friend,

The camel

For

Autumn comes swiftly

And with it

Your brokenness will end

Map

And where am I now?

Uncharted

A grid, unknown, and where I am now?

Childhood dreams, helium filled

And surrendered at midnight

Provoke or evoke

Their dissidence

And where am I now?

Breathing keeps

The corner of my lips

Smiling or straight

And where are you now?

Our footsteps echo

As we wander across this town

We're gently, floor struck, lying

Today's a new day

Or tomorrow's this day away.

YOU ARE

MADE OF

GOLD

Seventeen

Time it seems to me

It seems to me

Drawn out sighs

Between sheets

The sheets that needed to

Be washed last week

But "life happened"

And you forgot

Or promised to do it tomorrow

And time it seems

To me, it seems

Like red and blue

Flowing through my veins

Knowing I just

Can't remain

In the same place

With the same thoughts

Looking for daily grace

Seventeen

I want to hold your

Hand again

This time

For longer

Than the last time

When our worlds

Came crashing down

Or maybe it was just mine

I could remember if I tried

Time it seems to me

Oil paints

Disturbed suddenly

Without caution, colors smeared

And tears fall here or there

Tears of turpentine

Yes, the spirit of turpentine

Makes everything else cry

Seventeen

And drip, bleeding

Through borders

Once thought impenetrable

I will disclose the

The discourse

Of my heart

From the moment I saw you

I think it stopped

Beating

Or maybe I'm just

Tricking myself into

Believing

One of my many white lies

I still remember the way you smelled

Time can't take that from me

But I also remember the way she smiled

And the way her hair looked

Seventeen

Or their legs in those dresses

And sometimes time, it hides

These messes

Beneath opportune deliveries

Of newly drawn out soliloquies

I couldn't choose one

For the life of me

I've never been with one

Now and then, I'm choking

I come undone

But regardless

I couldn't choose one

For the life of me

And I surrender myself

To a waking calm

I couldn't choose one

For the life of me

Seventeen

But what would you have done?

I remember, for years,

Yeah years, you

Were the only one

Time blossoms

Cherry blossom tree

From atop

One day

I'll know you

Again

Don't Miss Out

Raw iron does not compare

To the weight that your eye lids hold

Bent, curving spine

Head hanging

Break the mold

Retract and desist

Lost in gloomy clouds

Of smoke and mist

Don't you dare resist

Every moment

Presented to

Despair, not care

Apathy's grip

Holds you tight

You know

Everywhere else

Don't Miss Out

They're smiling

And everywhere else

They're laughing

And other places, too,

They're enjoying

While you're looking at the sky

Alone in the grass

Laying in the grass

Alone at last

Missing out,

You know you are

On what they're all about

And then breathing

Becomes sporadic

For seconds, it's clear

You don't want to miss out

Don't miss out.

Don't Miss Out

You don't even know

What you're missing, what they're missing.

Ethereal charm

No harm in nostalgia

Until it drags you under

Torn asunder

Ever feel like you're the joke

No one laughs at

When you're around?

Ever feel like you're

The reason people

Crowd around and talk?

Ever feel like yours is the name

Everyone forgets,

The face people neglect?

Ever feel like there's more

To life than your sad, mundane

Train of thought?

You're not missing out on much

DON'T

LIVE IN

THE PAST

DON'T

BE

AFRAID

Change

So, what is change?

Comb my hair back,

I'm black and blue.

Add 10 pounds

Lose 21

My hands never

Knew the touch

Of someone

Who spoke the truth

But this will change

Or it will come

Undone

But, what is change?

Are memories

That linger

Change

Sting and burn

Are they an ideal?

Or, in reality,

All actuality,

Was I just as miserable

4 years before?

I'll change, I say

Every morning

With each new day

Oh, and I miss you

But our time

Was never gold

Never precious to hold

And now that I feel

The snow falling down

The mountain face

I feel my only choice

Is to scale this mountain range

Change

Failure surrounds me

Or so I feel

And I am no longer

Comfortable

Beneath my own skin

To cut it off would be

A delight, do me right

Muscles, veins, sinews

Holding tight

Or in reality

Would leave me a fright

People would keep

Further away

Still.

But It's

Psychological

Or I'm

Mythological

Change

And

Between A and B

All's chronological

But I'll change

A promise that can

Rearrange any current

Flowing north and

South, cardinal symbols

Speak

When I'm alone

The sky turns colors

The tree leaves

They whisper to me

But only those

At the top

When I'm alone

The ground begs my

Calloused heels to rest

Change

Upon lukewarm surfaces

When I'm in company

People surround

Oxygen and Carbon Dioxide

Hydrogen and H2O

Vibrate around me

Resound, my ribs

Forming a symphony

Around my beating, guiding

Muscle

I feel dizzy

Am I spinning?

Am I alone in this?

But change is constant

And I know I have

I know 2 weeks prior

I was entirely

Change

Apart

From 2 weeks later

Alone, my tongue

Cannot be trusted

It drones and mumbles

Certain, but changing

Its certainty, constantly

My homeostasis

Borders being

Extinguished

When a candle's flame

Flickers

A gentle breeze

Can only do harm

And I open my mind

My thoughts

Form sonnets

Searching in vain

Change

If only to find

Refuge

A place for myself

To remain

I'm a human condition

On the brink of extinction

And I know:

My internal revolution

Will only lead

To my

Evolution

LISTEN

TO YOUR

HEART

Set In Stone

Voices surround

Whispers

Or hushed

Remarks

Exclamations

Of love

And life

You can send your

Words of wisdom

Appreciation

Affection

Desire

Distaste

Or disdain

It couldn't matter

Any other way

Because voices surround

Set In Stone

More over

Plague

And even the exclamations

Become hushed remarks

In my heart

Even the words

Of appreciation and

Affection

Are known to be hollow

In my whole

Even the words of

Disdain and distaste

Flow past me

A polluted river

Still liquid

I won't let

You bring me down

This is set

In stone

THERE IS

TIME AND

IT IS NOW

A Little Bit Older

Don't worry about the present

Or do

Knowing you've thought the same

Years before knowing

That the present passes into the past

Don't worry about a thing

You are still young

But two years from now

You know you will be strung

Out thinking

The present of the past

Could have been used for

Or towards better

Things or people

When you're a little bit older you'll understand

A fish tank filled with regret

Doesn't harbor living fish

Currently Unavailable

Leave a message

After the tone

Even if we are

Facing each other

Get a needle

Shove it through

A rectangular piece of

Paper and write your note upon it

Now stick it to my

Chest, I'll read it later

Honestly, I might

Not read it at all

Once I'm cocooned

In hundreds of letters

Bloodshed, turned red

I won't have much time

[100]

Currently Unavailable

And you'll understand

Anyways

My scalp has been itchier

Lately; most likely

Because I laughed at you

When you said

You had dandruff.

Karma is harsh.

My skin has felt dry

Lately; probably because

I spend too much time

Touching it, making sure it's soft

Only a stone's throw

Ago, my body was a capsule

Open and belated

I can't say I know

Where I am

Where my bare naked

Currently Unavailable

Knee caps cast their shadows short

I'm currently unavailable

But know I'm still here

You won't hear my voice

Stricken with grief

Or a suppressed laugh

Burst from my chest

You most likely

Won't hear much at all

I saw a man looking

At me last night;

I watched him watch me.

He didn't stop

And it made me uncomfortable

So I stopped. Turn my face

Over my shoulder

As I walked away,

To see if his eyes

Currently Unavailable

Were still upon me

And they were.

It made me want to disappear.

You won't hear much at all

From me from now on

All of those dreams

Like clouds and hot air balloons

Have found kinder breezes

Or maybe they're just waiting

For me to follow through

But I know I cannot do this

I cannot invest my heart and time

In emotional pipe dreams

This perhaps is all you ever were

I met a woman the other night,

She blushed as her eyes

Met mine

I didn't blush.

Fearfully Afraid

"Meaningless" embodies

So many means

Of tragic, personal response

Hurtful despondency

Lurking in night's shade

Howls at your door

Meaningless moments

Pile up

Dirty dishes

In your kitchen sink

Scatter heart

The world bears

No bounds

Your feet are

Fearfully Afraid

Pools of molten lead

Leave

Cleave to those around you

Leave

Those around you

Are you

Are you breathing?

At your bedside

Window shut

Are you breathing?

Sleep

Calmly, gently

Unabashed; angelic

Shoulder sided

Caress and correspond

Only in dreams

I'll scream

Curls of my hair

Fearfully Afraid

Interwoven between knuckles

Blood shot

Drought plagues lifeless

Or barren worlds

Wounds

I could go on

More or less

I couldn't go on

Much longer

Than this

I'll shout

If only you'd

Respond

I'll despond

Either way

I'll go my own way

A path full

Fearfully Afraid

Of hands free

Hands pursuing

Serendipity

Fate

Has failed me

As of late

But I'll

Arch, twist, and turn

Yearning never

Felt so much

Like fire

Like life

I'm Only Going To Say This Once

Your words

They strangle and stir

The strangest of emotion

Seemingly

Beyond the reach of your

Vast complexion

Your ideologies

Quick spoken apologies

All asides

Rid myself of your

Darkest nature

You're sure to hide

Are you

Were you ever

Close to my bosom

Dear one

I ask

I'm Only Going To Say This Once

Tender one

Were you

Are you ever

Near my heart beat

Free, tortuously

My heart beat

How it beats

So rapturously

Your lies

Snakes and coiled

Ready to strike

I've been meaning

To tell you

Several times

Before

I'd been bitten

Too many times

Poisoned and sour

I retreat

I'm Only Going To Say This Once

For health

I impede on your

Versions of rational thought

All selfish quips

That help you sleep

At night

Alone

Or with her

Or her

Or her

All hers

All nameless

All great loves

Possible loves

The truth is

They're all nameless

And dirt

To you,

Of course

I'm Only Going To Say This Once

Only to you

I've been

Four people before this

I've been four

Manifestations

Of my souls greatest

Desire

And I grow and mutate

Any given day

The way a doppelganger

Uses cunning and logic

Wisdom of four

Years since passed

To prove itself

A clever shape-shifter

But you

Were always shapeless

[111]

I'm Only Going To Say This Once

The worst form to take

Liquid and dark-glow Morpheus

The destroyer of dreams

Too many times

To count, pronounce

I begrudgingly

Neigh, I say

Desperately

Attempted to fill your

Form with skeletons

Of kindness

Friendship

Love

Forlorn feelings

Quite queer

Bones with words

Seared upon them

Old runes

Of good intentions

I'm Only Going To Say This Once

But these bones shatter

Like glass

Every time

Your shadow passes

Past my bedroom door

For

(And I will only say the once)

You were always in it

For you

And you voiced your "you"

Every single day

A grackle singing at sunrise

Hands to the ears

A grackle sings at sunrise

I was never perfect

As imperfect as they come

A stain upon bleached linen

A belated apology

A soft shouldered sigh

I'm Only Going To Say This Once

I had never meant

To hurt anyone

In any way

Shape or form

I'd hold my head low

Disappear beyond bellows of

Steam rising

From the tea kettle

Tea for two or three

Food for two or three

I'll only say this once

Your voiced dissension

For my lack of conviction

Or raised applauds for "all you do"

For "never wanting you to be you"

Well it's all I did

Cleverly hid

In smiles or sweet words

I'm Only Going To Say This Once

For you

Because broken backs,

Of which you lacked,

Of which I had come to

Inherit only one,

Because broken backs

Are capable of only doing

So much

Of harboring

Or showing so much

Without running risk

Of snapping in two or three

But I did it

Gloriously, I did it for you

And material luster

Poured forth

From your charity

It was all you could muster

That material luster

And that was yours for me

I'm Only Going To Say This Once

But I was never in your flock

I was never like thee

Perhaps there were times

I wanted to be

But I was never

Like thee

And now I sound

Internally resound

A cry of glory

That has yet to come

For on the horizon

The future's horizon

I see the glory already

Spun

And I want to say

With breath and force

You were hurtful

From day one

I'm Only Going To Say This Once

A sack of bricks

Unmovable

Shalom

I was distantly alone

We were two brothers

Twins of one another

Though another may never see

A fiery passion, the glorious passion

That blazed within you

Or me

However,

And I'll only say this once

Every moment

Your tongue did snap

And correct me for my wrongs

You were wrong

And every time

You never understood

I'm Only Going To Say This Once

The warping ways of wood

You would leave bundles

In the sun

Covered in morning dew

Undone

Undo

You would leave it in the sun

Time, it correlates

Whenever one instigates,

With every time since passed

But let us

Reflect

365.242199 ways

365.242199 days

In a year

For this time tomorrow

And all the tomorrows that follow

I'm Only Going To Say This Once

I'll leave you in the clear

A hot air balloon

My love for you

Oh, how it once was

A vessel of travel and growth

But worthless to you

Though you'll never

Make it clear

Admit it out of fear

But you're a different class

I'm gold you're brass

Though I'm treated like lead

And you like a diamond

In the rough

Soon you'll see

The heart of me

Bloody and swollen

The heart of me

I'm only going to say this once

Weight Weigh Me Down

Weight, weigh me down

Heavy, sorry shoulders

Hang low, hang high

Surrender, remember

Calmly flowing currents

Running waters once dry

Desert, engulf me

Sand in my mouth

White-washed inner thoughts

I'm a lonely stranger

A lowly face amongst many

And every black hole

And every binary star

Are all made naught

All unwind

Weight Weigh Me Down

Unravel

And I apologize,

Like a summer breeze,

Dancing trees

Leaves, colors change

They rearrange

Like times since passed

Times held true

Tender, dear

Or forgotten, erased

Painted over and over

On the bathroom floor, tile dry

Ceiling spins above

I cry

Fingers grip wall

And sink

This running water

Now babbling brook, I'm in the desert

Truth In Tell-Tale Lies

I'm sorry.

There, I said it

And if you couldn't hear it

Perhaps refused,

Well, I wouldn't blame you.

Remember when

It was just you and I?

By the water's edge

We were stranded

Bewildered

Outspoken

Remember when

It was me and the sky

Me and the purples,

Truth In Tell-Tell Lies

Pinks and orange.

Yellow lit loudly

Mountains high

I remember,

As a child

I'd play in the clay

With my brothers

We'd play in the clay.

I remember how

Not every time since

But how

When we were kids

I would weep

Against the white wall

Adjacent to the door

I'd weep

When my brother,

He would leave me alone

Truth In Tell-Tell Lies

Off with another

Somewhere to be

Oh, how he would leave

Me alone

Distant yet faithful

My glorious brother

Oh, how he would leave me

Alone

Align these words

I remember the night

In that pick-up truck

My second time

To be stoned

And how the stars

They blurred

Like oil paints

Smeared, hard pressed

Truth In Tell-Tell Lies

Yeah, I was in the truck

Bed, we went 50

In a 30

My eyes, they were glued

To the sky

And the day

By the cave

When we smoked

In sheets

You, on your knees

Your invisible violin

Your words

Spelled out

Just how you cared

And I was worthless

For how many years?

4 or 5

To be exact

Truth In Tell-Tell Lies

My personal fears

I screamed at you

How I yelled at you

I jumped on you

Left your town

With two black eyes

People were worried

I'd done it to myself,

I said.

They were worried more

Or still.

I left her

Well

I left her

Whole

Or so I thought

When I left her

For you

Truth In Tell-Tell Lies

Who are you?

Dark and sinister

Mister

Who are you?

When I shower

I cower

And fear

For my life

So, who are you?

No longer do

My drains stain red

No longer does

My blood shed

Down my arms

Heart and arteries

Are whole

But who the hell

Are you?

Truth In Tell-Tell Lies

And why

When I cry do I blame you?

And where the fuck are you?

And at night

Nameless as all

I can barely walk

I stumble and fall

I was on top of the court house

You to my left,

I remember the height

Of it all

Afraid

Like me,

You'd tumble

And fall

If time was a river

Shallow, it'd be

Truth In Tell-Tell Lies

If time was a river

I'd be swept away

Or how I let myself be

Taken with the current

The waves concurrent

With my desire to leave

Oh, how I found you!

In such a mysterious place!

Oh, how I found you

Such surprise on your face

The top of the stairs

I remember it still,

Going to smoke

I had just finished

Put my cigarette out

With my heel and foot

Truth In Tell-Tell Lies

And you to go smoke,

I ascended those stairs

Ascended in spirit

Ascended those stairs

Oh, how I found you!

Amidst a city so strange

My first time

Capturing its skyline

Its streets.

Oh, and I found you

Random at best

But lost you

I lost you

And I don't

Even know

Who you were

Who you are

Oh how I found you

But I never did know you

Truth In Tell-Tell Lies

Oh, how I find

Time

Time to think about

You.

But I really don't.

Time to put you

On that high chair

Time you put you

Higher than I

I can't reminisce

It hurts, oh,

It hurts.

And when I look

In the mirror

I see bruises

Yes, bruises.

Truth In Tell-Tell Lies

Another, I met

Between fire

I don't know

What to do

And honey

Doesn't help

No, not one bit.

I'm left here

I left

And truth

Like the tortoise's shell

It keeps me

Heals me

It keeps me

High and dry

Remember

Oh, you remember

Truth In Tell-Tell Lies

You and I

On that beach

Yeah, I was there

When I was six

Oh, I truly was

How strange to think

I took you there

Yeah, that same beach

But you stood there,

That same shore

As I

How the waves touched,

Caressed

Though I never

Undressed

I didn't know what to do

A virgin

Truth In Tell-Tell Lies

Bright and blue

The bird that sings

Caged

The bird that sings

In a cage

No, I don't know what to do.

We'll travel,

Travel the world together. We'll see wind and shore,

We'll travel it all together

Because loneliness can

Only

Be spread so thin.

If I know you,

Whoever you are;

I am

Wandering

I am wandering

The World Is Shrinking

Fire side

The world is shrinking

Fire side

The world

He breathed her last breath

Only

Mother Earth was never mother

Unless you look close

Enough

In vain

One might approach

A thought so close

To boast her tranquility

Look closer

To know

He sits by the fire side close,

Mother Earth,

He sits

The World Is Shrinking

Eating pomegranates

Or figs

He sits on mountain range

Forest or grove

He sits

On wind washed

Ocean, beach, coast

Mother Earth

Pregnant, momentary birth

Of all that

Shall come

Shall arrive

More over,

Mother Earth

Her whimper at sunset

His palms

Fast pressed

One word

Could surmise

All seasons

The World Is Shrinking

All autumn mornings

Watching the sun rise

Although Mother Earth,

Her echo lost in

A clearing green, splendor

Holds your magnifying

Glass

Mother Earth,

He calls upon you

He once was

Is now

Will be

Mother Earth

He is she

However

She is he

From Whence You Came

Misty mornings, a cool drift

Time that turns and you're standing

Feet barren, neck exposed

Frozen, and you're shaking

Childhood laughter lifts

Then drifting back away

Towards thunder and lighting

In your mind

Your neck with no protection

Because that night you choose to forget

Took it away

In the hands of regret

You don't, though

Regret or dwell, you sail passed it all

On a swell of self

From Whence You Came

Your brothers and yourself

You see them clearly

Christmas Eve and you're laughing

Shared bedroom and bed

You speak of what you

Expect Santa to bring

Other than mom's or dad's smiles

Their pats on your head

And then it's gone

Feet barren, neck exposed, you're walking

Throughout the mist, all grey

Sea-like or something you'd

Expect to see near the ocean water's waves

You forget where you're going

Only briefly remembering where

You came from

Ask Me

Morning tide when

The air is sweet and

Light, you're glowing

What do you want me to say?

I know nothing about life?

Okay, I'll say

I've said it

I'll say it again

I know nothing about life

I would have gone to the vet

I would have picked up the cat

Before they put him to sleep

I would have washed the dishes

And the cleaned the room

And stopped drinking

One beer short of drunk

Ask Me

I couldn't have fallen so deep into the current

That hand holds or foot holds

Were far from me, beyond my reach

But none of this would have plagued you, anyways

And if the saying is true

If one is to know me from my actions

And not my words

Allow me to say

The saying is false

I deserve benefit of the doubt

The same doubt that clouds your day

And keeps you locked in the same routine

Every second, minute, week

The faces change, the names change

But they're all the same

And it doesn't make the slightest difference to you

So fine

I don't know much about life

But in my dreams

Ask Me

I've built a place

Where I don't have to know it all

And I don't flow away, heeding the river's call

And we bask beneath the sunlight

Fearless of the fall

(or lack thereof)

All the coffee cups, sweet sugary things

Make our means to life

And we smile

More than I could muster within this waking life

If you wanted me to say that I don't know anything about life

Well, I haven't seen it all and I don't but for the record

I would say anything you wanted me to say

If I felt

It was right and surrounded us with light

Coffee cups

And those sweet sugary things

Maybe that is life

Our words exchanged

Ask Me

And rearranged

Maybe that is life

I would say it

If it brought me closer to you

I painted a picture

Several days since passed

You gazed at me from every brush stroke

Fairytales

I believed in love

Tender beauty smile sweet

I believed in love

Cold reality as called

By the crowd of strangers

In the night or day

Strangers on their way

To God knows where

That cold reality

Pulled me under deep and now love

Seems but a distant dream

For in all I see more/less than love

It quickens me, sickens me

All is when push comes to shove

I used to believe

In you and I

Yet inevitably realized

Fairytales were all written in books

Fairytales

And before that, passed around

A sailing cloud, traveling

Through the word of mouth

And for all of this

Though the tales survived

Not once did their stories

Ever come alive

Measure

Measure days by the sound

Of the hour hand ticking away

Or the sun making moments nostalgic

Measure days by the dollar or how tired you are

As you lie down to sleep at night

Or measure days by grace

All that you learned and the number of smiles

That played across your face

Laugh when you can

Because there are those that can't

And love as gently as the light shines down

Measure your days or don't measure at all

But be thankful that you lived to see another

One day, the measure of days, weeks, years as well

Will mean less to you than everything you have forgotten

For that reason that you can't quite remember

Don't measure your days at all

Everything will be okay

Compass

Somewhere language is instilled, created

Be still

Speak oceans and I will be your waves

Language, words and every kind can say

What needs to be said

Whisper water and I will be your earth

Oh, how I need your rain

Close my eyes to see

The colors, a spectrum most tried and true

Cerulean emerald sheen

Flashes of neurons firing

Fire smolders, it had your color

I know it sets you free

I'll listen to your lament on cracked cement

Deep in summer's heat

Compass

Of all that has come undone

Mention mountain peaks and I will be your evergreens

Eternal life and glowing

Christmas year round

Language holds me down

Wanting me to say more

Find the words and do more on foreign shores

Passed the sea, I mumble maps beneath my breath

Nearly out of sight

If you'd just be my compass

I'd be your summer breeze

Mongolia

The earth frozen

My breath bearing testament to the warmth I harbor inside

I breathe in and out-back again, I breathe

Snow falls on all- ice is a blanket singing of cycles

With every crystal that falls from the sky

My heart, feathers flying, falls as well

And home is far away

I think of you

Warmth as powerful as flame

My aim, I pull my arrows close and breathe

My blood and kin, back again, I wish to see their smiling eyes

Christmas bells and tidings of winter form crystal castles in the clouds

I want to see their smiling eyes-a gift I cherish on the steppe

A step towards happiness

My shivers calm my thoughts and sighs

For you a gift within my ribs

You're the one that sets my compass free

☾

Here

Days when I know myself

Thin veil over my body and soul

See through silk screen, a print from you to me

Flower patterns or snowflakes free

Fall from thick grey clouds surround

And sail throughout our skies

See no sun, come undone or drift slowly down

The rivers bend

I'll tell you when and where

Our words pitter-patter like rain

Lift like smoke

Signals become clear

My hand grows weary

A solemn sigh to realize by and by

I want you near

I am far, far away

But I want you here

Sinking Into Suburbs

I don't want to do this anymore

This sinking into suburbs

Tame trains of thought built up like houses

Each, all the same

Inhabited, dilapidated

I can't do this anymore

Sadness takes its toll

When there's no reason

To be down

"But you'll soon come around"

I tell myself each dying day

Invest in my future

In hopes poised on when and where

And you know I just want you near

But we don't exist in each other's pockets

My wine glass is full

And I can't do this anymore

Sit in silence, protected well from the cold

Sinking Into Suburbs

But we're suffering from global warming

Or so I've been told

Our ice bergs are melting, becoming one with the sea

Salt in our wounds

Saying, "These are your mistakes"

And the magpies take more from you

Then you care to remember

But you can't say I didn't try

So I go to sleep at night

Solemnly hoping one day

I just might

Find my key forged for the sole purpose of setting my spirit Free

Brother

Childhood, laughter shared between those

Who should matter most

Now several years since we've seen each other smile

Spill your words across my canvas

Blank and in dire anticipation for your perfect pigments

Cleverly placed

A display of heart and soul and all those reasons

You never called or visited

You could go a few miles away

And still not manage to say "hi"

A passing "goodbye"

As you travel on your way home

But if it's for the best

My lips are sealed

I won't weigh you down

With my appeal

As to why I feel things should be different

Was it the mistakes I made?

Brother

How I delayed

My family's functional growth

Or how I hurt myself

Time after time

A travesty to behold

Well, those nights spent by myself were my own to endure

And if you couldn't help me

Then hold the fear that I'd do it again and again

Why stay farther away still

Your Dove

Related to those thoughts

That bear down

Break or make your fall

Are those sweet scented flashes of light

Against clouded, hazy ignorance

Though far from bliss, like steel bars and iron wool

You're scrubbed clean of your past

And become a caged bird

Sing, they tell you, sing

If not one more song then two

But these are not those thoughts

Only distantly related, vaguely similar

Like all stones are at the bottom of a pond

All frogs that croak can't be counted one by one

You can see the bordering mountains

But not what lies beyond

They are those kinds of thoughts

Your Dove

That seem almost the same

They are glittering beauty

A wonder to behold as their mental stories unfold

Only for you

That is the cage, what grasps you at night

And in broad day light

They lure you with thoughts of love

"Yes, think of your dove"

Young, dearest one

They slide their hands against your face

Like warm summer rain

"Yes, think of your dove and think of your love"

"Of all that is true and pure"

And then they leave you

A bird in their cage

They won't ask you to sing

And you couldn't if you tried

Just lie down and be quiet

This will only hurt a bit

Tell Me

Tell me please, he said

Christmas lights by our side bright

Like candles glowing without flame

The truth poured out from my mouth- I didn't quite care

Though I've heard one should beware

Lest the truth carries too much weight- and it left me cold

Almost empty, I couldn't place why

Until I realized it was in his eyes

"We'll have to agree to disagree" was all he said

"Oh, but it's my life"

And with every other analogy

Apology, he tried to set things right, take flight

Away from that scene

It stayed with me, though- it stuck to me

Like barnacles or benevolence

It was on me and I left

I dared not let myself abandon

What is true for me

Take Me Anywhere

Whisper, haphazardly

Softly and silent

We are alone so my ear is your

Mirrors couldn't reflect what was shared

Is given from me to you

I accept your offering

Of poetic eloquence, innocence

In that moment, brief

Come with you

You ask me to

Hold the door open

"The choice is yours"

You stand still for but a moment

The kind that lasts for centuries

And what is all of this to me?

I ask myself because you told me to

I'm black and blue still

From years since passed

Take Me Anywhere

Hesitation, light precipitation

Come with you or stay

Await another day

To gasp and shudder

Adore another vision specter's form

Adorn with lies and ideas of what I prize deep within myself

I say "you can take me anywhere as long as it's far from here"

Without care or convalescence

The future is bright for those without calendars, wristwatches, and pocketbooks

Time is no one's fool

Sublime

Everything in-between

Still remains to be seen, heard, felt

A flutter, doves' cries

A morning song for all who care to listen

Ave your surrender

The slate is clean and a rush rises

Passed knees and thighs, over rib cage, knuckles, eyes

Smile quick, a moment's disposition

My malnutrition and heavy glow of home

Your wandering thoughts led you here

Loved and dear

You'll be taken care of

I had promised you

Or said to you

I was trembling deep

Let's enjoy the sublime

Passed our prime

And all that lies before those mourning doves

Sublime

I thought they sang for you

Abandoned child wrapped in anything but

And say to yourself

That you are golden splendor sweet

Ambrosia, I'd drink you if I could

But I'll hold you close instead

Forest grove and mountain's chill

It's the first day of the rest of our lives

Sour Milk

That feeling you get

Realize their flat out lies

And revert to your inner sanctum

When their kindness curdles, sour milk and maggot meat

They still expect you to smile

And will hold you accountable

If you do not

Will not

Put on that happy face

Don't show your distaste

Or consider how you've tried

Friendship for you is love deeper than skin

Something that couldn't, wouldn't

Treat others "like that"

If it tried, breathe

Slow and deep, don't fight

It in your mind

Wait for a sign on how to react

Sour Milk

Distract the pain that has formed inside

Calloused, near cold

Just break the mold

They don't have to know how much it hurts

Youth

Face on the floor

Revolving door in my mind

Thoughts enter and exit

Streaming back and forth with my attention span

And all of those plans I once devised in youth

My youth still quivers

Clings to me

A child that has no home beyond his skin and ribs

The other on the ice, walking

Without another in sight

I silently hope he does not fall in

But am distracted yet again

With thoughts of countless

"you's" and when

All those times stacked up to the sky

My mind is my ladder

I don't want to climb

Out of breath but with all of the time in the world

Youth

Faces resonate, replicate conversations once shared

Was I ever really there

And who is that in the mirror?

Let everything rush out, rushing in

My hope is my hand rail

Out of breath I breathe

My childhood scream and fears like dark shadows

Liquid death swims beneath

That hope, a light

Beacon begging bright

I gave him my canticle despite my procellous blood flow

Scarlet flood through veins and bone

Hold me, hold me

Call me home

I wish to see your face with flesh

Though I dare not ask your name